Tango of the Widow

Tarla Kramer

Tango of the Widow

In memory of Edi Antonio Omonte Torrico

Tango of the Widow
ISBN 978 1 76109 644 0
Copyright © text Tarla Kramer 2023
Cover image: Tarla Kramer

First published 2023 by
GINNINDERRA PRESS
PO Box 3461 Port Adelaide 5015
www.ginninderrapress.com.au

Contents

The hairy hand of fate (autumn)
  Life Without E   11
  The hairy hand of fate   12
  Eleven o'clock   13
  Plane Trees   14
  Help   15
  Dexamethasone   16
  Omens   17
  Lifting Machine   19
  TV   20
  Lost Cause   21
  Letting Go   22
  The phone call   23
  No Credit   24
  Morning has broken   25
  The Funeral   26

Exposed (winter)
  Cycle   29
  Magical Thinking   30
  South Wind   31
  North Wind   32
  Counsellor   33
  Odd Shoes   34
  A dream   35
  Hope hides in unexpected places   36
  Coorong   37
  Marriage   38
  Exposed   39
  Crow   40

Garden	42
Setback	43
Things that bring dread	44
Dodgems	45
Autumn Leaves	46
Church	47

New Shoots (spring)

The White Van	51
New shoots	52
Blossom	53
Toothbrush	54
Goals	55
Pond	56
New era	58
Anniversary	59
Shadows	60
The fucking brick wall	61
Walking Through Mud	62
Three years on	63
Acceptance	64
Edi's garden	65
Hoarding	67
Pink daisies	68

Born-again virgin (summer)

Cardigan	71
Opposing biologies	72
The last one	73
Libido	74
Computer's Broken	75
Say no more	76
Little white lies	77

Sour Grapes	78
Chiropractor	79
my bladder my betrayer	80
The South African dentist	81
Thinking back	82
Dreams	83
Somebody that you used to know	86
Acknowledgements	87
About the author	88

Let not the flood sweep over me, or the deep swallow me up,
or the pit close its mouth over me.
Psalm 69:15 RSV

For the Lord will comfort Zion; he will comfort all her waste
places, and will make her wilderness like Eden, her desert like
the garden of the Lord…
Isaiah 51:3 RSV

Thou hast turned for me my mourning into dancing; thou
has put off my sackcloth, and girded me with gladness.
Psalm 30:11-12 KJV

The hairy hand of fate
(autumn)

Life Without E

I was young and had to go to Bolivia.
For its music and not its food. It was okay.
Found folks in Bolivia a bit shy.
Although it was good to not shoo guys away constantly.

But in six months I found my man,
who was a muso.
And not a bad husband. Hubby and I had four kids.

In 2008 my husband got a brain tumour
and that was that.

The hairy hand of fate

We've been owner-building six months
when the nails start falling
out of Edi's left hand.

Then his left leg won't step properly.
'Get checked,' says Jacky V,
seeing him limp.

As soon as those two words leave her mouth
it's here and our fate is sealed –
the rest is formality.

At the doctor's he has to touch
the doctor's finger which is easy
then his own nose, which he misses.

The doctor's face says it all.
The rest is formality.

Eleven o'clock

At eleven o'clock my husband has
an appointment with a brain surgeon

Eight years ago today he had another
eleven o'clock appointment

That one with a minister
and his wife-to-be

And after today's eleven o'clock
appointment with the brain surgeon

We'll find out if there will be
any more anniversaries

(written on the bus at 10.40–10.45 a.m, 3/6/08)

Once en punto

Mi marido tiene cita con una neurocirujana
a las once de la mañana

Hace ocho años atrás como hoy tenía otro cita
esta vez con un padre y su futura mujercita

Hoy, después de su cita médica
vamos a saber si habrá más anniversarios

Plane Trees

As we plough through
the weeks of diagnosis –
an MRI plus two biopsies –
the plane trees on Frome Road
drop their leaves.

There is no glory in this ocean of brown
and it's relentless, still going
when the radiation starts.
And there's a leaf in the hospital lift
the day my husband gets his death sentence.

Help

A local handyman named Quentin
comes to our rescue.
He's heard about
the tumour
the five kids
and the unfinished house.

Do you need help?
I gabble an assortment of words.

Do you need help?
He had cancer himself
and God healed him.
He can heal Edi too.

But none of that stuff
has any bearing on
the outcome.

When Quentin brings
his band of churchmen
it's the day to day help
and the cheer, watching the
heart of our home take shape,
that gets us through.

And when everything goes pear shaped later on
he takes in my stepson.
These are the works
that won't be burned.

Dexamethasone

When can he stop taking it?
I ask a doctor
It makes him so hungry
his face so fat
he's not who I married but a toad.

The doctor looks at me
wondering what planet I'm on
whether I was born yesterday,
that sort of thing.
There's pity in her face
as she explains that he can't –

It's a permanent thing in his impermanent life.

Omens

The power is off the day we move into
our not-yet-finished dream home
because someone called Matty hit a stobie pole and died.

And we have to dump our mattress which is mouldy
from being on the damp floor of our temporary dwelling.
It feels unlucky to throw out our marriage bed
but we can't keep it.

Three days later Edi goes to bed mid-morning,
which is not like him, but he's not feeling that well.
He feels zero per cent and wants a little lie down.

While we put boards beneath the windows
he could feel himself slipping.
But I wasn't listening
you'll be fine, just have a rest.

By midday he's gone
doesn't remember where the kids are
or where to pee.

I call a nurse
she thinks the dexamethazone will help –
he missed a couple of days –
but it doesn't bring him back.

It's a grim old day, probably my worst
and dread on my face when I get the kids.
There's no one I can call.
The night is long.

In the morning Edi doesn't even know whose house it is,
but Raymond from church pops by and saves us
with a cheerful greeting and how beautiful the day is.

I concede it's an attractive day – can't do better than that.
He stays with Edi and tells him stories
about his Queensland childhood
while I run the kids to school.

Then I take Edi to hospital.
Kevin notices he doesn't look too good
and he struggles to remember his own name.

Leaves by mortuary ambulance eight months later.

Lifting Machine

Lifted from his hospital bed for showering,
my husband swings at a perilous height.
Put me down! he cries like
some early movie heroine.

He has the King Kong of brain tumours:
Inoperable, grade four
and is not the hero
any more.

TV

It's January
middle of the afternoon
I sit next to Edi in his hospital bed

Jim is in the other bed watching telly; sport is on
a woman analyses a netball match
and what they could have done better

and I weep for us,
so far away from
that kind of normal

Lost Cause

i

when we can barely drag ourselves to see Edi any more
my mother goes in with seedless red globe grapes
and feeds him

ii

it's been ages since the nurses put on music for him
but when he rounds the final bend
they put the music on again

Letting Go

The chewed-up food dribbling down Edi's mouth
and sagging eyes tell me he's going to die.
It's only taken him a year. The hospital
has been his home for eight months, during
which his English has improved. But since Christmas
he's slowly receded. He's in there somewhere
but I can't see it. Praying for recovery is hopeless now.
Just wish I'd not wasted time commanding his tumour
to go away – it's not taking any notice. Instead I go home
and like Jacob, wrestle with God until dawn. As the sun
gets up I have my answer and am ready to face the unfaceable.

The phone call

After saying goodbye to my husband
and sending him to his mother in heaven
we go home.

The kids are hyper
like someone's just died.
To occupy myself
I plant things.

Each news break
I turn my head
and hold my breath.

Then at 6.50 p.m.
just after I've served dinner
the phone rings.

It's the doctor.

No Credit

We file into the darkened hospital room
where he lies

Tears roll down Enzo's cheeks
but the rest of us just gawk
and whisper

When they have gone out
I stay behind and poke his cheek
It feels weird

Then out the corner of my eye I see it
The sheet moves
like an exhalation of breath

The undertaker tells me
it's a trick of the mind
that I'm not going mad

When I use the hospital phone
to call the plumber for our hot water system
there it is again

Morning has broken

on my first morning as a widow
I'm up before the sun
and pace the garden

a Chinese pistachio I planted a week ago
has changed overnight to a pinky autumn red
a gift from above

I plant the goji berry I wanted to put in yesterday
but was saving it for the occasion
then it got too dark

a crow perches on the outside dunny
that Edi and Dad built last year
says gark gark gark
I know, you don't have to tell me
it flies off

the little falcon which hunts the block
watches from the TV antenna
Hi Edi I tell it – it too flies off
and now hunts the block next door

for three weeks I get up at dawn
sit on a plastic chair Edi got at a garage sale
and drink tea in his just-planted garden

The Funeral

There are hugs.
Lots of hugs
but no tears.
I want to weep a bucket
but am numb.

The kids kneeling
by the hole
chat to each other,
watching the
coffin go down.

Exposed
(winter)

Cycle

After the adrenalin of death subsides
I wake each morning to stomach-retching panic

somehow I make it through the day over two hurdles:
get the kids to school and get dinner

evenings are better apart from the early darkness
no curtains hung yet except in bedrooms

and the blackness is so overwhelming
I crawl into my cave

there I put on Bolivian music
and cry into my Sudoku

I go peacefully to sleep
then it all starts again.

Magical Thinking

A new Andean music CD
almost carries me back to Bolivia
where I met Edi.

There's a part of my brain
that thinks I'll find him again
if I go now.

I'm almost gone myself
and feel like I haven't been here.
Not in Quorn.

With the kids, yes
but barely here apart from that.
I put the CD away.

South Wind

On the coldest day in weeks
I'm out there in the wind – gale force at times –
thanks to the Southern Ocean cyclone.

With a pick and shovel
I put rocks into place by the house
building the retaining wall
Edi was about to
when he got sick a year ago.

He would have been muttering
from up there all this time
at how long it has taken me to start
but better late than never
better alive than dead.

It won't be no Sachsayhuamán
but it makes the house look solid
and helps me feel safe.

North Wind

When the north winds blow and plants curl up, so do I –
15/8/2009

north wind blow
dry the ground
dry my eyes
dry my tears

north wind blow
take my breath
take my pain
take my strength

north wind blow
make cats hide
make chooks shelter
make farmers tense

north wind blow
stir up dust
blot out hills
like nothing exists

north wind blow
turn sky red
sometime bring rain
but not today

Counsellor

a counsellor visits
the tears come as soon as he arrives

we sit in the garden
which isn't a garden yet but bare earth

and a few newly planted things
we smell the boronia 'Heaven Scent'

a few weeks later
he sends *The Grief Map*

as if it were something I could use
to find my way out

by then he's changed jobs
and I stop progressing

a year later the boronia's pungent smell
brings back pungent grief

when it died I felt relief

Odd Shoes

it's like forgetting a child
doesn't seem possible until you've actually done it

I've done a good morning's work
but have to go to end-of-term assembly
to see my kid get a certificate

ten minutes in
my guts begin to sink
as it dawns on me my feet feel different

I look down
there they are
one brown boot and one black one

serves me right – so swept up in my writing
I cared not about mundane things
like whether my shoes match

I slide them off my feet
wrap them in a jumper
walk out in socks

as for the certificate that was just a fuckup
nothing materialises except awkwardness

A dream

I drive on a rough road
into the desert
a new tyre bursts
and a blue steam train comes past

then I find an orchard
of young citrus trees
and each sapling
has two huge fruits.

Hope hides in unexpected places

the first glimmer
when Isabel and Amaru race each other
to me in the car.

The sky is dark clouds
with the sun trying to peep through
before an inch of rain falls.

But hope and happiness
are in the kids' smiles
as they look at each other and run.

Coorong

I find my anger driving by the Coorong.
In that place good for hermits, I scream
and cry at the top of my lungs

and tell things to fuck off
like Woods Well and Policeman's Point,
Century plants and a drum letter box.

But the thing I'm most mad at
is a sign that says 'Honey'

I don't want their fucking honey!

Marriage

Had some stupid idea
that I could 'get' another husband
it would be easier than losing parents or kids

Another stupid idea I had
was that it's easier
when you know they are going

Turns out I just didn't get it
we fitted so well
once I'd worn him in
I forgot I was wearing him

Now I'm naked
have nothing
no strength
not even faith in life.

Exposed

There are certain people
skilled at measuring grief

I meet one at the rest stop near Dimboola
when I pull up for free coffee and biscuits.

He sees my van full of excited kiddies
and in two questions has uncovered

why I'm on holiday with so many small kids
and no man.

It's not the first time a curious older man has been that efficient –
a campesino in Bolivia comes to mind –

and I wonder who these men are – what have they
been through that gives this pain radar

and I'm learning there's no such thing
as a free coffee.

Crow

at the cemetery
by an old broken grave
one is dying

a funny kind of omen
the death of death perhaps

is this the end?

The still small voice:
you *will* get through this
you *will* get through this

Garden

There's an act of hope in planting
so I struggle on wasting hundreds of dollars
of free money from the government
buying plants that ultimately die.

When this dries up
I do cuttings instead
and some live for a time
but drought gets them in the end.

Where I live
nothing takes over
simply replanted
after all else is gone.

I'm only left with tough ones
and mourn the many losses.

Setback

It doesn't take much –
a trip to Adelaide
stickfast fleas on the chooks
or a birthday –
and I'm back in the dreaded morning Cycle

can't breathe
gag on food
sweaty palms
and the delicate hold on sanity

as months pass
and the Cycle eases
I start to welcome it
like an old friend.

Things that bring dread

Mother's Day flowers
in the shops.

The early darkness
of June.

Carpets of capeweed
in early spring.

Jenni riding by
on her horse.

Even the feel of the air
on my skin.

But worse is the sound and smell
of the hospital doors opening.

These things take me back
where I don't want to go.

Dodgems

I was once the kid
with the guy on the back
that Seinfeld described so well
but 20 years of driving helps.

Now I'm flying
nothing can hurt me
nothing can stop me
or my wild laughter.

Autumn Leaves

Late this year
as if the trees got together
said 'don't remind her'
and stayed green.

But when we get to Laura for the folk fair
Tony says 'didn't Dad die a couple of weeks
after we came here last year?'

And the trees
kick him under the table.

Church

Is always soothing when you're the walking wounded.

Although it hurts to hear Marg rave on
about how God healed her husband
while mine lies in his grave.

But when Quentin's cancer comes back it's even worse.

Then God does something
weird and takes Quentin home
on the sixth of May also, 365 days later.

Death be not proud
Ha ha ha ha ha ha

New Shoots
(spring)

The White Van

The owner never knows
how much hope I've sunk
into this painter's van
that I've looked for it each morning for years.

Waiting for it to come up the valley
on the way to Port Augusta.
Rejoicing if I catch a glimpse
on its way back home.

The sight of it tells me
that somewhere life is normal
that all shall be well
as long as God gives another day.

New shoots

after the suspense of mid-autumn
new shoots bust through crusty earth
eager to live

before winter ends
I try something new

line dancing lifts my heart
into a new realm
after harsh pruning

Blossom

it's still winter on my block
like in Narnia

things blossom elsewhere
in Adelaide and at Anne's
or sprout leaves
but all I have is buds

T-shirt weather comes
but winter winds drive the mildness away

even after spring arrives
hail cuts my purple irises to ribbons

Toothbrush

Does Edi still have teeth
Maya wants to know –
his toothbrush
is still in the drawer.
Of course he does.

But in the shower I think about
what the rest of him might look like –
visuals I can do without.
Only his teeth would be intact
from that big smile which drew me in.

Goals

When the lady at the bank
asks me what my goals are
I don't have an answer –
getting through each day doesn't count

Goals – what are they?
I barely remember having any
apart from SURVIVE

In the coming days
I try to make some
but I've forgotten
what I once wanted

(Don't laugh
but it's seven years
before I can book
a holiday in advance)

Pond

I

There's a hole in the garden
from when Edi made adobes
But instead of filling it in I buy black plastic
which stinks out the car and makes me stop and check the tyres

Then I add water
Isabel and her friend Toni
add themselves

Dave gives me duckweed
which brings dragonflies
We get tadpoles and sedges
from Waukarie Falls

Insane evaporation in November
means I need shade cloth
(which blows off in a storm)
Catherine gives me water plants

Our older cat drinks from it daily
the younger one falls in
trying to catch frogs

II

frogs are singing
as summer turns to autumn
their happy sound helps
through the floods cyclones earthquakes tsunamis of 2011

life becomes humdrum again
and I make good progress on the garden
but never get the frog song back

a white-faced heron devours them
it still haunts the block

New era

I have a new cycle now:
inspiration desperation frustration peace

it starts when I see Sharon's stunning garden
then return to my sad little patch

I want it now
a proper pond
a low stone wall by the roses
a curving wall around Edi's garden
700 Trees for Life trees
pavers and paths
my carport up
the big green slide in place
veranda erected

I'm showing Sharon all these things in my head
knowing it will be years

Next week she turns up and starts hauling rocks
gets me started
and one day the garden in my head
is outside.

Anniversary

The second one
is almost as bad as the first

The thing that keeps me upright
is making a cake for Marg
(which a dog bites while she's out)

So Sharon comes
starts me on the next wall
shores me up.

Shadows

At Weeroona Island
clouds come up from nowhere

Back home
rain not forecast
is falling

The fucking brick wall

I

and there it is again
out there waiting
for me to get distracted

poke my head out –
that's when the brick wall comes out of hiding
and laughs evilly

I learn to stay in
there is safety in my torpor

II

the brick wall is in cahoots
with the tipping point

which gets further away from me
as time goes by but is still there

you don't realise of course until you begin to tip
and go smack on the ground

Walking Through Mud

another winter of the soul day
a thick blanket of cloud
has reduced it to greyness
where yesterday was all blue

it is still
my heart heavy
the house a mess
tears are close

I'm as heavy and slow
as a wounded beast

I'm not wallowing
just going through grief's bucket list –
like look at his CT scans, those envelopes
in the cupboard that repel me –

and with each thing ticked off
the weight lessens
the mud shallower

Three years on

and the little falcon watches me plant trees

first it's perched on the outside toilet
that Edi and Dad built
then it's on a fence post all fluffed up

are you ill, I ask it

then remembering I used to imagine it was Edi
look up and it's gone

no it's not

it's on the big green slide –
the one we got the day before we found out about the tumour

Acceptance

is realising that even in marrying Edi
I made a hash of things
and if I'd gotten the one I wanted before
things would have been worse.

No longer do I walk in wistfulness
of women who still have a man –
I'd have pieces to pick up whoever I married
and had they lived or not.

There's still one more step
on this long hard road
and that is refinement through fire –
more on this later.

One day when
the grief monster up and leaves
life almost empty
the universe hears a request for more crap

and the next monster dump truck of life pulls in,
the load already lifting
to bury me in five weeks' time –
more on this later.

Edi's garden

i

There's a curious thing
I've noticed in the garden
that if a plant is
accidently trodden on
soon after being planted
it grows up stronger
does better than the others
this is heartening indeed

ii

I love the rain
wish it would come every year
but in the drought
as the earth is stripped back
old things that were lost,
buried, forgotten, emerge
and beg to be dealt with

iii

Edi's garden is grown now
there is iris, jonquil
eremophila, quandong, wallowa
a hedge of safety for the cats
and kangaroos
who come at dusk
to drink from the pond

iv

we plant dreaming of the future
and once growing we get joy from the past
'remember when there was nothing?'

a photo of dust and junk from the early days
brings greater joy
than the fulfillment of the dream

Hoarding

Here lies
my husband's toothbrush
on the ground
outside the door.
He doesn't need it any more;
he's dead.

Besides
his teeth are fine
up in that boneyard,
and haven't needed cleaning
this past ten years.

I should throw that toothbrush out
but don't.

Pink daisies

in the gentle light of autumn
the girls catch me crying over
pots of pink daisies at Tinline Plants

they don't understand the tears
shed by their silly mum
and laugh

but I'm lost in a dozen autumns
and the dozens of plants
I bought along that road

and the hope I felt each year
getting going in the garden
before the dread and fear

most things planted then are dead and lost
like the pink daisies from Nana Jean
along with the tough years, they're long gone

but not those little ladies –
they're huge –
no longer babies

Born-again virgin
(summer)

Cardigan

sexuality on the eve of menopause
is like wearing a cardigan
you can't button up

Opposing biologies

Diagnosis time
and Edi's biology is going
'I'm going to die; procreate NOW!'

unfortunately mine is like
'he's going to leave me with all these children
it's not a good idea!'

and I don't want to know about it
until it's too late.

The last one

He comes to me three times while I sleep
Twice in the first month
Once more six months later
on the anniversary of our meeting

On the first visit
we are on a bus in Adelaide
and can only kiss

But on the second visitation
I wake up grinning

It's the culmination of a rogue thought
from when he was in hospital
with no hope of recovery –

we had not yet done it
for the last time

Well now we had

Libido

Sitting by the fire
when something unrelated on TV
reminds me of sex, a thing
I'd pushed to the furthest
corners of my mind,
pretending it didn't exist.

And then I think of how it was.

Computer's Broken

Get your scrawny butt around here PC Man
and fix it
No I would not like help
over the phone
It's been too long since your last visit
I'm tired of sitting here alone

Say no more

God's ok
with
wanking
if it's
done discreetly
and you
never talk about it
ever.

Little white lies

I am NOT attracted to you Mr
Personwhoshallremainnameless.
It's just that an annoying piece of hair gets in the way
whenever you're around.

It seems to flop in my face the moment you walk in the room.

So don't be misled
I actually think you're annoying
and certainly don't have a crush on you.

Sour Grapes

she needs a root
say the married ones
to the widows and divorcees
even though they aren't getting much more
and probably wish they didn't have to

Chiropractor

Manhandled by the new practitioner who
holds me in ways I've not been in a decade.
He swings my legs across the table as if I
were no more than a recalcitrant infant
prolonging a nappy change. After forcing out
a swearword he steps back to admire his
handiwork. Anxious to please I ask if I should
continue the foot exercises set by the
previous chiro. But he's already lost interest.
'If you want' he says, mind elsewhere.
It's not like I'll be seeing him again.

my bladder my betrayer

pressing on some nerve and causing chaos
returning me to my long dead husband
but sometimes not

one night it flies me to Ecuador
into the arms of my old friend Pablo
who I didn't quite sleep with 26 years ago

another time it takes me back further to Peter
the guy who said I needed a cock up me when I was still a virgin
who I also didn't quite sleep with when I could have

that bladder of mine says, Hey Pete, remember how you said
I needed a dick up me when I was still a virgin but I didn't
realise you might have meant yours and therefore didn't take
you up on your offer to relieve me of my virginity later in the
year? Well actually I was wondering if I could you know, now
that it's been over a decade since I lost my hubby and I'm a
virgin again

and just when things are going pretty good my
sub-conscience goes (ACCESS DENIED) what the hell are
you doing WARNING! WARNING! he hasn't broken up
with his girlfriend!

The South African dentist

is gone now
I remember his kindness
made me cry
the first time I went
reminding me
what it was like
to have someone to look after me

Thinking back

of all the men
I was hot and cold on
an expert at the blow-off
I saved many of them from embarrassing themselves

although a few were led on the merry dance first
except for one bad one who was hot
I suppose I was quite wicked
in my unpredictable way

But there was a someone
I was never cold on
who somehow knew me
understood me deeply

despite language and culture
he knew exactly how to play it
so I never got bored
you know who I'm talking about

RIP Edi

Dreams

We're going at it in the back room of my friend's old
monastery in Albury
when Mum walks in
then I wonder how he survived and got normal again.

We're on a bus
I'm remonstrating with him for not sticking around
for even a decade of marriage.

He's laid out on a table like in *NCIS*
instead of a nose he has two holes
of a shot-off face.

He's wearing his brown jumper for work at home
which ponged
but I just hug him breath him in.

At the hospital he's made a full recovery
his hair still short
he's even lost the hospital smell.

He's come back from heaven and yes
Quentin was there
Great! He can sort out the shed!

He's bought a little motorbike
we take turns riding
then I kiss him outside the kitchen
and say Merry Christmas.

He's living in some other town
where he went for work
I don't have his address or phone number
no way to contact him
am deserted and alone.

He's survived
proved the doctors wrong
is well and still with us.

We're back in La Paz
we've left the kids at home
so we can party if we want.

He's bugging me about things I have to do
so I shoot him in the chest,
blam blam blam and shut the door
I better do something about it
before the smell gets me in trouble
but I don't want to open the door or dig the hole.

We're in old carriages at the Pichi Richi Railway
and I'm devouring him
but feel hurt and bewildered
I've not seen him much lately
have to hide from my parents that
I don't know where my husband eats or sleeps.

He's not dead after all but alive and well
and living in Kangaroo Island where he's fathered a daughter
to a neurotic Filipina he's no longer with.

I wake at 3 a.m.
the divorcees were right!
thank God he's dead.

Somebody that you used to know

don't tell the Christian widow
that at least you'll see him in heaven

if she's read her Bible she knows
we're like angels there

the marriage is over
and should you spot him

it's like bumping into someone you were once married to
somebody that you used to know

Acknowledgements

Some of these poems were first published elsewhere: 'Lifting Machine' in *Cordite Poetry Review*, and 'Morning has Broken' and 'Pink Daisies' in *Inscribe*.

Thanks to Aidan Coleman, James Cooper and my fellow Tabor students for their encouragement, to Ray Wood for his help with the manuscript, and to my daughters Isabel and Maya for their input. Thanks also to Juan Garrido-Salgado for his help with the Spanish version of 'Eleven o'clock'.

I would also like to thank the people who helped, supported and prayed for us during the circumstances that led to the existence of these poems, especially Quentin and Margaret and the people of Flinders Christian Fellowship; my mother, father and stepmother, Jacqueline, Sharon, Marie and Bernadette; Stewart and Yvonne; the people of Quorn; plus online support groups for the widowed, where I found brothers and sisters to traverse this chapter with.

I am also grateful for the existence of the written word, and found much comfort in those early years reading the following works: the Bible, *The Waterlily*, *Burning* and *Playing with Water* by Kate Llewellyn, *The Year of Magical Thinking* by Joan Didion, *When Will I Stop Hurting – Dealing with a Recent Death* by June Cerza Kolf, *The Young Widow's Book of Home Improvement* by Virginia Lloyd, *A Grief Observed* by C.S. Lewis, *Cleo* by Helen Brown, *A Widow's Story* by Joyce Carol Oates, and *To Live Again* by Catherine Marshall. I hope others will find solace in these pages too.

Many thanks to Stephen Matthews of Ginninderra Press for his patience with this newbie author!

About the author

Tarla Kramer grew up in Adelaide and now lives in the Flinders Ranges. Since graduating from Tabor's Creative Writing Program in 2019, she has had poetry published in *InDaily*, *Cordite*, *Borderlands* and *Inscribe*. Her manuscript Odds & Sods was one of three winning collections published in *Friendly Street New Poets 21* in 2020. Her chapbook *poems for the non-compliant* was published by Ginninderra Press in 2022. *Tango of the Widow* is her first full-length collection.

When not sitting in her writing hut staring out the window, she can be found staring at screens in her various day jobs, or staring out of the guard's van on the Pichi Richi Railway.

www.ingramcontent.com/pod-product-compliance
Lightning Source LLC
Chambersburg PA
CBHW071024080526
44587CB00015B/2493